Junk Drawer

Junk Drawer

Poems by

Michael P. Hill

Cover design by Shay Culligan
Collage by Michael Bristow
Photography by Sawyer & Harmony Hill
Digital repairs by Andrew Hill

ISBN: 978-1-63980-014-8

Kelsay Books
502 South 1040 East, A-119
American Fork, Utah 84003
Kelsaybooks.com

This collection is dedicated to the three best first draft readers gathered under one roof: Katheryn, Sawyer & Harmony.

All my love and appreciation,

—MPH

Acknowledgments

Some of the poems in this collection have appeared or are forthcoming in the following publications, sometimes in slightly different forms:

Briar Cliff Review: "Wind Farm"
Concho River Review: "Instinct"
Connecticut River Review: "Boats"
Dunes Review: "Faded Tattoo"
The Flyfish Journal: "Heron"
Gray's Sporting Journal: "Reading the Water," "Church"
High Shelf: "Handkerchief"
I-70 Review: "Night School," "Dowsing"
Lucky Jefferson: "Train Town"
Making Waves: a West Michigan Review: "Old People in the
    Grocery Store"
Midwestern Gothic: "Kinnickinnic," "Team Mom"
Opossum: "Cassette Tapes"
Plainsongs: "Silver Screen"
Pomme Journal: "Anniversary Poem"
The Sea Letter: "Party Line"
Soundings East: "Record Store, Greenwich Village"
Star 82 Review: "Detasseling Corn"
Stillwater Review: "Home for Lost Poems"
Stonecrop Magazine: "Junk Drawer"
Third Wednesday: "Birds of North America," "Catch," "Roofers,"
    "At the Veterinarian's Office," "Books on a Shelf," "The Night
    Tom Petty Died," "Lake Fishing, East Texas," "Street Scene"
Tilde: "The Tire Swing Dreams of Summer"

Contents

It took me years to get those souvenirs.
—John Prine

Everything is somewhere.
—My Mom

Junk Drawer

Though not exactly large,
it still contains multitudes,

something I'm reminded of
every time I wrestle it open

in search of one essential item
or another like, say, a checkbook

or a nine-volt battery, maybe
a clothespin. And when I do,

I never fail to be amazed
by what else I discover:

old cell phones, headlamps,
an emerald green glass ashtray,

tiny screwdrivers, rubber bands,
an uncoupled walkie-talkie.

Surely, I think, there's a poem
in here somewhere.

Party Line

The dead-end road
that I grew up on
was out in the country,
where backyards gave way
to woods, and woods to fields,
where fences were formalities
and neighbors shared phone lines,
where sometimes, expecting a dial tone,
you'd put your ear to the receiver
and instead find small voices,
at once familiar and foreign,
transmitting confidences
you might well have intercepted
had you not had the courtesy
to lower the handset
and gently hang up.

Birds of North America

Perched always on the verge of flight,
this ruffled old field guide
was never one to collect bookshelf dust,
not with pages this accustomed to a good fluttering
from the likes of my ornithology-inclined grandma
who, according to the inscription, received it as a gift
from my great aunt in 1983.

Both of those old birds having long since flown
from this life, it roosts on my shelf now,
still at the ready should I need to put a name
to some curiously-plumed backyard visitor,
not unlike my grandma and great aunt,
each of whom once took me under her wing
and showed me how to see the world.

Reading the Water

At daybreak,
the tall grass beaded
with silvery dew,
I crack open the cover
to a crisp, new page
of river and wade on in,
following along closely
as riffle, run and pool
spill their stories,
each one a unique narrative
filled with boulders, overhanging branches
and undercut banks,
but all flowing to the same conclusion:
the telltale rise form of a feeding trout,
its meaning rippling outward
into the morning,
where I grasp firmly,
strip out a bit more line
and ready my cast.

Night School

There was knowledge, albeit
of a darker sort, to be found
in those dingy Midwestern bars

where our teenage cover band
offered up imitations of Elvis,
CCR, Pink Floyd, John Cougar

Mellencamp and so many more.
Fact is, the Agate Inn, Foxhole,
Blarney Stone and any number

of other smoky, dimly-lit dives,
dark rooms that they were,
were the places we developed,

our identities fluttering slowly up
out of that murky emulsion.
On Friday and Saturday nights

we'd lug a small music store's
worth of gear into and back out
of one of them, and reel off

as many as four 45-minute sets
for the dancers and the drunks
in between. And then, sometime

around closing, we'd settle up
and leave that shadowy world
of adults to return to our lives

as everyday high school kids,
a little smoke still in our hair,
a little night still on our breath.

Catch

The signature smack
of the ball in the webbing,
cowhide on leather,
might just be the best part
of this passed-down pastime,
one that arcs all the way
from my baseball-rich childhood –
the trading cards, the trips to the ballpark,
the tellingly brief little league career –
and across the intervening years
to this warm summer evening,
where I take it and hurl it on
like an heirloom, over the lawn
and into my daughter's waiting glove.

Roofers

Materializing in the soft, gray glow
of morning, a small flock
has come to alight atop a house
across the alley. Like woodpeckers,

they drum out intricate rhythms
through the early hours, their busy music
echoing about the neighborhood
as they pry up and turn loose

the old shingles, scattering them to the air
like tumbling blackbirds. No sooner
have they stripped the roof bare
then they begin feathering it anew,

their voices raised in birdsong
as they call, respond, and call again
to each other along the downslope
of afternoon. Once they're done,

they drop from their perches
to tidy up the shingle-littered lawn,
then take flight, their wingbeats receding
as a dusky quiet descends.

At the Veterinarian's Office

He was a big fellow,
had to duck just to get in the door,
and long on swagger, with broad shoulders
squared firmly against the day.
But when the vet's assistant appeared
and handed him the small metal cage,
empty save for an old, threadbare pillow,
I saw him start to cave in on himself,
his voice catching in response to her questions
about cremation options,
and his face pinched by the weight
of unexpected grief, as if the emptiness inside
the pet carrier was growing heavier
by the second, and it was all he could do
to keep holding on.

Kinnickinnic

(pronounced ˈki-ni-kə-ˈnik)

Standing thigh-deep in the Kinnickinnic River,
I lean forward, watching the drift
of my dry fly so intently
that I can see clear back to my childhood
and the pages of my dad's old *Fishing Facts*
magazines, splashed as they were
with the same sorts of tableaus
as the one I now find myself occupying.
Back then I was bent on untangling the mysteries
of trout streams, this one in particular,
and had no inkling of all the other existential snarls
that would soon enough divert my course.
Tonight though, with the early June twilight
silhouetting the leafy crowns of oaks and elms
and the hungry trout boiling the surface
in the mad frenzy of the Sulphur hatch,
I am filled with a sense of arrival. And the river,
right here where I left it, welcomes me
without reservation, offering up
eager tugs and dazzling aerial displays.
Yesterday my son caught his first trout,
a gorgeously mottled twelve-inch Brookie,
on a different fork of this same river.
It was also his first fish taken on a fly rod,
and the smile it brought to his face is what I expect to find
when I lift my landing net from the dark water
and get a look at the joy wriggling inside.

Faded Tattoo

There's a tarnished iron cross
on the leathery left arm
of the man in line at the store,
a faint blue brand receding
into liver-spotted skin. And
there's a bright red something-
or-another on the pale thigh
of the girl in the cut-off shorts
wheeling by outside on her bike,
her life still out in front of her
and no reason I can think of
for it to occur to her that
nothing is permanent, not even
the sun spilling its bold inks
across the darkening horizon
before it slips out of sight.

Team Mom

She used to take us to see the Twins
at the old Met Stadium, long torn down now,
home plate buried somewhere beneath
the Godzilla-like footprint of the Mall of America,
where I imagine lots more moms
probably take their kids today. But back
in those pre-Metrodomian times, my mom
would load my brother and me up
in her long, low-slung Ford wagon and sail off
down I-94, and then I-494, toward Bloomington,
where the Minnesota Twins hosted their opponents
out in the open air. One year she even got us there
on opening day, only to have our repair shop loaner
die on us in the parking lot. I don't recall
how much of the game we saw or missed, but I do
remember being marooned out in the middle
of that endless, pot-holed sea of asphalt,
no cell phones for another twenty years, walled in
by more cars than I could begin to count,
and looking up at my mom, secure in the knowing
that, however it all panned out, she would find a way
to get us where we needed to be.

Books on a Shelf

Like old pals, they lean on each other
for support, a close-knit clan
swelling with stories
for anyone willing to look
past the dust on their jackets
or the must on their breath.

In fact, I'd like to think
they're not simply content
to keep to themselves, but rather
that they'd gladly open up
to whoever might want to drop by
and sit with them awhile.

At any rate, they don't get out much,
not anymore, so here they rest,
among friends, lingering on
past glories as they index the days
before their pages were dog-eared
and their spines were bent.

Train Town

Neighbors have been whining
of late about the trains
blowing their whistles as they pass
nightly through town.
To their ears it's a nuisance,
but to mine it's a comfort,
the same as it's been
in all the other train towns
I've lived in down the years,
where the deep exhalations
of determined locomotives
suggest the spent sighs
of fellow travelers, lamps trained
on the dim landscape ahead
as they push on toward home.

Handkerchief

My grandpa was a handkerchief man,
not sure I ever saw him use a tissue.

When he felt a sneeze coming on or
if it was just time for a good honk,

he'd reach into his back pocket and,
like a magician, flash a bright bouquet

of floral print fabric, quickly tend to
the matter at hand and then, as deftly

as he conjured it, make it disappear.
He was a tidy sort without much need

for anything he did not already have,
and he even tied a handkerchief onto

his bald head when he pulled weeds
out in our garden, one loose corner

lifting gently in the breeze like a leaf
or a petal on a flower as he blooms

once more here in the warm sunshine
of memory, perennial as the summer.

The Night Tom Petty Died

In a drizzling rain
beneath a cold and starless sky,
some nine thousand of us
drew together,
in spite of our better judgment,
to warm our outstretched hands
over the communal crackle
of an open-air rock concert,
our collective breath
fogging the night
as ribbons of sound lifted
from the stage below
and turned to smoky echoes
that curled up and away from us
into darkness,
imprinting themselves
on eternity.

Detasseling Corn

Early on a summer morning, the world gone cool and sparkling, the school bus would drop us at the edge of a field, where we would emerge, weighed down with sleep, water jugs and lunch coolers, just to be swallowed up by a great green ocean of head-high seed corn – wave on wave of stalks standing ready for our soft, young hands to uncork the feathery tassels from the tops of each plant. All day long we'd tramp those leafy corridors, shirts damp with morning dew and necks reddened by afternoon sun, facilitating cross-pollination for three-and-a-half bucks an hour, our fourteen-year-old imaginations flush with the possibilities made real by a season's worth of earnings. Soon enough there would be drivers' licenses, social lives and after-school jobs, but for the time being there were muddy sneakers, bouts of corn rash and the occasional aerial attack, tassel spears raining down on unsuspecting heads followed by retaliation and a discharge of laughter, as we soldiered on toward the end of our Midwestern childhoods, the future burning holes in our pockets and the landscape revealing little as to what lay beyond.

Lake Fishing, East Texas

The flat, breeze-ruffled surface
conceals another surface below
and a secret world in between

where, with the aid of a fly rod,
I maneuver a hook half-hidden
beneath a ribbon of fiber and fur

as though it was a kite on a string,
twitching, tumbling and gliding
through a tranquil, indifferent sky

not unlike the one here overhead,
with its vast and silent depths
and its sleek, torpedo-shaped clouds

all schooled up like so many bass.

Instinct

My childhood dog Ginger lived in terror
of thunder, fireworks, gunshots and all manner
of bangs, booms, blasts and thuds.
When summer storms rumbled overhead
she would tremble so profoundly
that no amount of comfort could reassure her,
try though I did. Of course, I'll never know
what sort of imagined pursuers chased her
through those difficult hours, bellowing
at her heels all the while, but tonight,
as our quiet street comes under attack
by a rogue battalion of firecrackers,
it's more of the same old heavy weather,
so I gather up the small dog here next to me
and clutch him to my chest as he shudders,
jackhammer-like, the air about my face gone hot
with his panting. And, while I am well aware
of his propensity for flight, not to mention
my inability to soothe him, I keep him close,
even as he struggles against me like a sprinter
anxious to be out of the blocks, powerless to resist
the sharp report of the starting gun.

Home for Lost Poems

...best of luck finding a good home for your poems.
                        —from a rejection letter

At the home for lost poems,
ill-conceived ideas and insufficient inspirations
take up residence alongside slipshod sonnets,
abandoned acrostics, ham-handed haiku,
probably-should-have-been prose poems
and all manner of free verse flounderings. Here,
hidden away from the world, they find acceptance
of another sort, turning their wayward phrases
in the company of fellow outcasts, free to write
their own endings, arrive at their own conclusions.

Record Store, Greenwich Village

There's barely enough room
for all the records,
let alone any customers,
but my son and I
edge our way in anyway
and quickly take up positions
at separate bins, riffling through
the shiny, cellophaned album jackets
like they were pages in a flipbook
on the history of rock'n'roll.
Every so often I pause
to inspect one that looks promising,
then resume my search for an LP
worth getting excited about.
Glancing over at my son, nearly 15,
I'm struck by a likeness of myself
at the same age: clear-eyed,
the whole world at my fingertips,
ready for something good
to flash into view.

View-Master

Among children's toys
of a certain era, it's notable

for the ability to transport us
beyond our surroundings,

its eyepieces like windows
opening onto other worlds –

desert savannas, rainforests,
theme parks, moon landings –

brought squarely into focus
via slender cardboard disks

and stereoscopic 3D images
so vivid and immersive that

the effect was not so unlike
that of a scene from childhood

revisited through the lens
of a poem, depicted, it's hoped,

with enough color and depth
to properly bring it to life.

Dowsing

My father-in-law moves slowly,
elbows at his sides, forearms
parallel to the ground. His hands,
meanwhile, maintain a loose grip
on two slender, L-shaped metal rods,
each pointing straight out ahead,
as he makes his way forward
through the calf-high pasture grass.
Fixated on those twin instruments
of divine guidance, he watches
as they start to turn toward each other,
then stops when they cross, x-marks-the-spot-like,
over the site of a buried water line,
or at least the presumption of one, arriving
as he has at a point beyond explanation
located at the intersection
of belief and chance.

The Tire Swing Dreams of Summer

In the lonely backyard
of winter, the tire swing
hangs silent and still,
tired of trying to strike up
conversations with snowdrifts
who never respond anyway,
and pretty much immune now
to the neighborhood squirrels,
who just walk all over her
like she wasn't even there.
With nothing else to do then,
she dozes off, swaying in and out
of vivid, full-color dreams
where she sails rider after rider
through a bright kaleidoscope
of untethered delight,
the sun warm on her sidewalls
and the breeze in her treads
as she glides by and by into waking,
and then just to find herself
shivering and shrouded
by a heap of new-fallen snow.

Boats

On the glowing, fold-out screen
of memory's slideshow, my dad
nearly always appears with or within
a boat – a rowboat, a bass boat, even

a canoe: a fleet that launched him
out into the wide channel of his days
and sailed him so swiftly across
an abundance of waterborne years,

only to maroon him in the end –
no boat now, just an empty space
in a drafty garage where a vessel
used to be moored, and a cane

to help him navigate the hard surface
of this strangely solid new world,
one last oar for him to pull on
as he steers for the far shore.

Wind Farm

As dusk settles on Iowa,
the big blades of the wind turbines
turn dutifully, the whole crew
having clocked themselves in
for the night shift. Like pale sentries,
each with a blinking red eye,
they stand watch over the plains
as they rake the sunset-stained clouds
stacked up along the horizon,
spinning them steadily
into bales of starlight.

My Daughter, Practicing the Cello

Sound slithers out
from under the closed door
to her teenage bedroom
as she winds her way slowly
up the serpentine spiral
of a scale, her horsehair bow
drawing long notes out
of the instrument the way
a snake charmer's flute
uncoils a length of cobra
from a woven basket,
coaxing it out bit by bit
and then easing it back
down the way it came. In
and out of keys she glides,
ascending and descending
and, ultimately, distilling
the oft-venomous world
of an adolescent down into
an orderly series of notes,
something she can exercise
some control over and,
in time, even tame.

Silver Screen

A wintry matinee morning
and the front room picture window
has framed in the action outside so that
it looks like a black-and-white film.

The movie has something to do, it seems,
with snowflakes confetti-ing down
as cars and trucks alike shoulder into
an antagonistic north wind and

shivering rooftops wrap silvery stoles
about them to keep out the cold.
The plot is a study in contrast
that builds to a sparkling finale wherein

patches of ground, once dark and exposed,
don luminous ivory gowns,
each one as stunningly glamorous
as any that I've ever seen.

Heron

Truly a master angler,
the hardly inconspicuous heron
stalks the shallows
on silent stilts,
its bowstring neck drawn taut,
sights set on the moment
when it suddenly shoots
down into the current
and emerges with a wriggling fish
scissored in its beak.
Just downstream, caught
up in the action,
I let my rod tip drop,
summoning a missed strike
and a jolting reminder
of where I stand,
knee deep in the flow,
a fledgling fisher, clearly
winging it.

Anniversary Poem

for Kathy

Shoulder to shoulder
in the uncluttered morning,

two coffee mugs
converge in the kitchen,

ready to be filled
with another day, the same,

my dear, as you and I:
two vessels given to warmth,

transformed as we were
by the tender kiln of a love.

Cassette Tapes

At the bottom of the closet
in an old Mr. Coffee box,
they live out the rest of their days
in silence. Their technology inferior
and all but obsolete, they're still bitter
over the whole compact disc thing,
though it sounds like it won't be long
before those flashy interlopers
wind up alongside them. And
while their old running buddies,
the vinyl records, managed to come back
out of the closet somewhat recently,
they know better – despite the rumors –
than to go and get their hopes up,
not with a format so clunky and frail
and only slightly more reliable
than that of the lowly 8-track tape,
the last of which left here
what seems like ages ago
for the landfill.

Singer

Ann Rebecca Neuhoff Griffith, 1940-2020

Silent for some time now,
my late mother-in-law's sewing machine
whirs back to life under the steady hand
of my daughter, who's loaded the spool pin

and is carefully guiding a piece of fabric
beneath the foot presser, the needle
high-stepping with renewed purpose
as she leans into the floor pedal, drawing

not just thread up from the bobbin,
but also memories up from the past,
and affixing them to the willing material
of the present, where the familiar hum

of the old motor suffuses the room
with something like a hymn, mending,
stitch by stitch, the split seam between
this world and the one to come.

Old People in the Grocery Store

It's easy enough to pass judgment
but, really, who hasn't been lonely enough
to want to tell the guy behind the fish counter
how you used to catch those shrimp
with your toes in the Long Island Sound
when you were a boy, or ask the produce manager
if he got to go to Hawaii to pick those pineapples?
You might even find yourself so starved
for conversation that you inquire of a stranger
the location of the "prescription aisle"
just so you can point to the frozen treats
in the case behind you and say with a wink,
"sorry, looks like I just found it."

Church

Sunday morning
and I'm headed up the canyon road,

a stained glass sky spilling sunlight
onto the high rock walls,

their jagged spires
thrust heavenward.

Below, beneath vaulted boughs
of cottonwood and pine,

the river's rush of voices
collides in song

and a fisherman opens his fly box
like a hymnal.

Street Scene

At the far end
of a summer day,
dusk bearing down,
pale slivers of sunlight
stripe the deep green
of our limb-shadowed lawn
and, just down the block,
a man in a white T-shirt
stands out in his yard
and soaks it with a hose,
water streaming forth
like the beam of a flashlight
searching the soon-to-be dark
for the hours gone missing
while, across the intersection,
a woman scrubs a beige minivan
with a faded yellow sponge
that she dips in an orange bucket
of soapy water, her vehicle
glowing softly in the gauzy light,
offering up what seems like,
at best, a half-hearted defense
against the steady advance of night
as a pair of bicyclists rolls past,
followed shortly thereafter
by an inky blue pickup truck
presumably hauling off
what's left of the day,
darkness trailing
just behind.

About the Author

Michael P. Hill's poems have appeared in *Midwestern Gothic*, *Briar Cliff Review*, *Gray's Sporting Journal*, *Opossum*, *Concho River Review* and many other fine publications. He has worked as a journalist, toured and recorded with rock'n'roll bands, earned a Master's degree in Library & Information Science, and wet a line in more rivers, lakes and streams than he can possibly remember. He grew up in Western Wisconsin and spent meaningful stretches in both Texas and Washington before settling in Northern Colorado, where he lives with his wife Katheryn, their children Sawyer and Harmony, and their dogs Harold and River.

Made in the USA
Monee, IL
27 September 2021